A Journey
to Shanti

Photographed,
Compiled and Edited By

Sylvio M. Tabet

Proceeds from this book will go to charitable organizations

ISBN No. 0-9654184-0-5

Publisher
Horizon Investment, Inc.
1877 Rising Glen Road
Los Angeles, CA 90069

To all the mothers of the world.

With Blessings and Love
Sri Sathya Sai

His Holiness the Dalaï Lama
9/12/97

"THE ENCOUNTER"

(translated from the French)

Two days ago, I gave my son a picture of some Buddhist priests
Underlining the red tunic of a child monk, hands clasped and pacifist

Today the dream is revealed, and it is the beginning of a new adventure
This encounter, totally fortuitous, foretells a marvelous future

What is it all about? It is about this surprise to which I responded intuitively
That made me say "compassion" with great joy, and instantaneously

He gave me a big smile and with a large gesture, He shook my hand,
The simplicity of His outburst reflected the purity of a child, and
The wisdom and love only a Holy man can convey
With the grace and splendor only a Divine presence can display.

Everything happened in the lavatory, and lasted just an instant
An instant that was the infinite and the absolute, endless and omnipotent.

It was at Rome's airport, the Eternal City,
We were taking the same plane, direction India, the spiritual country.
He was there to brush his teeth, very unconventional,
I was there longing to relieve some needs, very natural.

What can be more banal?
But far from being usual,
That was the encounter, presage
Of an intersidereal pilgrimage
In the depth of my soul's desire
To fuse with the purity of His fire.

Kaboom!

It was in the most incongruous place that I touched the Mahatma,
It was there, in the most unconventional way that I was touched by the grace of
His Holiness, the Dalai Lama

Simply Thank You

On my way to Puttaparthi
9/12/97

To all the mothers of the world.

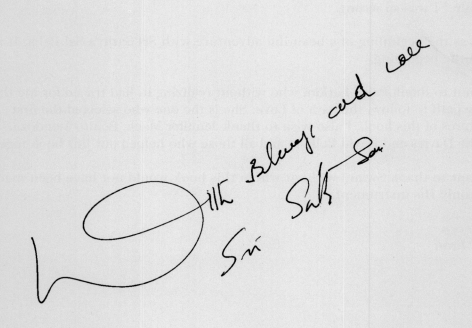

With Blessings and Love
Sri Sathya Sai

ACKNOWLEDGEMENTS

We were sitting on the beach facing the ocean. We were the only ones. A flamboyant golden sun was setting on the horizon and the infinity of the sea. She had me bring two glasses and a bottle of champagne. I opened the bottle, poured the champagne and we toasted. She said, "To a thousand sunsets."

I drank the Sun, I drank the Light.

The next day she brought me a book to read, "The Bridges of Madison County," and it was the end.

But not really—a few months later she called and introduced me to the "I Ching" and later on she told me that I should read "Autobiography of a Yogi" and then "The Celestine Prophecies." She looked at these books on the surface, but I dove deep into them.

One day, she came to me with the story of a man in India, who moves his hand, "like this" she said, moving her hand horizontally in small circles. "Poof," she said. He materializes a big diamond. "Poof," she said. "... And here is this beautiful diamond in your hand." I said, "This must be another fakhir." I was so wrong.

It was the beginning of a beautiful adventure with Sri Sathya Sai Baba. It is still the beginning.

I want to thank Paige Larkin, who without realizing it, had traced for me the only path to follow, the path of Love. She is the one who selected the first pictures of this book. I also wish to thank Jennifer Mack, Benito Mendoza, Chris Davies and David Bellfort and all those who helped put this book together.

I want to thank Swami without whom this book would not have been made. I am only His instrument.

Sai Ram

INTRODUCTION

I dedicate this book to all the mothers of the world. They are the ones who guide the child in his first step. The love of a mother is incomparable. A child is innocent. The mother's task is to preserve that innocence. Her Love is the best support to such a mission. When a child grows with Love, he will give Love and Love is the path to God.

Why this book?

Few people read the Bible or any religious text or philosophical books. They are either too long, too complicated, or too difficult to understand. And there are so many of them. Most of us keep such books in our library or our bedroom, opening them occasionally or not at all. But many keep beautiful pictorial books in their living room—coffee table books for the guests. We look at coffee table books, alone or with friends, comment on the pictures and sometimes read the underlying text. I want us to do the same with "A Journey to Shanti." The pictures will lead us to read the quotations of Sri Sathya Sai Baba. The quotations will tell us about human values and the meaning of life.

The basis of our spiritual life is given by our religion. Often we do not understand it or do not practice it. Often religion puts in us the feeling of guilt and sin—and our beliefs and actions are distorted. Sai Baba tells us that the meaning of life is enclosed in a simple word: DIVINE LOVE. *"There is one religion, the religion of Love."*

I hope that these simple quotes will awaken their curiosity to understand that there is more. All the quotes of this book are His. I compiled and edited them from His teachings. They remind us of the wisdom to include in our everyday activities and life. We read about the Christ, Buddha, Muhammad, Moses and many other saints. But how much do we believe in them? How much do we practice their teachings? They seem so far in the past. Sai Baba is present and gives us the chance to live the experience of all those who,—a few thousand years ago—encountered the messengers of God. It is not a coincidence that His followers are counted by the millions. For some, He is the incarnation of God; for others, He is a holy man; for still others He is a wise man. But nobody can deny that His Life is His message: " Love all, Serve all, Help ever, Hurt never." Sai Baba brings tremendous changes in the life of those who approach Him from near or far. He is the Divine energy omnipresent in each of us and His mission is to awaken the Divine power sleeping in each one of us.

By changing us, by changing ourselves, the world is being changed for the better. Our destiny lies in our own hands. Sri Sathya Sai Baba has changed my life and I believe—not because of my reading and my faith,—I believe because I lived the experience. I believe that *"Life is a Journey from I to We."*

I hope that every reader experiences the bliss of Divinity.

Sai Ram.

Sathya Sai Baba, the **Avatar** (Divine Being) of this age, was born November 23, 1926, in Puttaparthi, a small remote village in South India. As a child, He demonstrated exceptional qualities of wisdom, compassion and generosity. One example is that He would take His meals out of His parents home to share with the beggars on the street. When He was seven years old, He began to compose spiritual songs that were performed at religious festivals. Soon He began to materialize objects such as candy and pencils for His playmates. On other occasions, He would pick a variety of fruits from the same non-fruit bearing trees. To this day, Sai Baba materializes objects such as jewelry and sweets for His devotees. Most often He materializes vibuthi, sacred ash, which has healing and spiritual powers. He says: "My miracles are my calling cards. I give the people what they want so that they will give me what I want, their love of God."

When He was fourteen years old, Sathya Sai Baba announced to His parents and fellow villagers that His mission was to bring about the spiritual regeneration of humanity by demonstrating and teaching the highest principals of truth, right action, peace, love and nonviolence. He has stated, "For the protection of the virtuous, for the destruction of evildoers, and for establishing righteousness on a firm footing—I incarnate from age to age. Whenever disharmony overwhelms the world, the Lord will incarnate in human form to establish the modes of earning peace, and to reeducate the human community in the paths of peace."

Since 1950, Sai Baba's residence and headquarters have been His **ashram** in Puttaparthi which is called Prasanthi Nilayam meaning the abode of perfect peace. He is widely respected in India and has followers throughout the world. **Prasanthi Nilayam** is a pilgrimage site for spiritual people from all religions, cultures and countries.

Baba counsels many of the people who visit Him in India. Others seem fulfilled just by seeing Him. Many who have visited Sai Baba say His greatest miracle is His ability to transform them. Often people come to see Him with doubts and apprehensions and return home with love in their hearts, peace in their minds, and a resolve to live a more giving, spiritual life. He has said, "You have come to get from me tinsel and trash, the petty cures and promotions, worldly joys and comforts. Very few of you desire to get from me the thing I have come to give you, namely, liberation itself." Baba defines liberation as the realization that you are one with God.

Government leaders and educators in India hold **Sathya** Sai Baba in high esteem because of His efforts to raise the national moral and spiritual levels and to improve educational standards. Baba says, "Education must implant elevating ideals and kindle the lamp of wisdom. Character is the most precious gift of education." He has established an educational program that encompasses the kindergarten level through advanced college degree programs. He has built a university system for women and men that is accredited by the Indian Government. He has also built and oversees elementary schools, high schools and technical schools. There is no tuition for the students who attend these schools or the colleges and university.

Baba's schools teach a curriculum of science, commerce and the arts as well as a character education program called Sathya Sai Education in Human Values also known as Sathya Sai EHV. The Sathya Sai EHV program is based on the values of truth, right action, peace, love and nonviolence. Sathya Sai EHV stresses the importance of service to society and tolerance for people of different races, cultures, nationalities and religions. This Sathya Sai EHV program is being used in schools throughout the world.

Sathya Sai Baba teaches that selfless service is the highest spiritual discipline, and He exemplifies this ideal in His life. He says, "My life is my message." In India, Baba has built, staffed and maintained many hospitals including a Super Specialty Hospital in **Puttaparthi** that provides care and surgery for cardiac, ophthalmology, neurology and urology patients. Medical care in these hospitals is given free of charge.

Throughout the world, followers of Sai Baba have established Centers in which members study and practice Baba's teachings. These Centers engage in selfless service in their local communities. The Centers also offer devotional meetings with singing, meditation and prayer. **Sathya Sai EHV** is taught to children in the Centers as the *Balvikas* program, meaning awakening of the child, which is a spiritual education program.

"Let the different faiths exist; let them flourish and let the Glory of God be sung in all the languages ... in a variety of tunes; that should be the ideal. Respect the differences between the faiths and recognize them as valid as long as they do not extinguish the flame of unity. If each person lives the ideals propounded by the founders of their religion, unaffected by greed or hate, then the world will be a happy and peaceful habitation for man."

"I carry no labels assigning a country of origin or residence for myself. The entire mankind is my family. There is no one in this world who does not belong to me. All are mine. They may not call out my name, but they are still mine. I shall not give you up even if you keep afar. I shall not forsake even those who deny me. I have come for all."

"There is only one religion,
the religion of Love.
There is only one caste,
the caste of Humanity;
There is only One Language,
the language of the Heart;
There is only One God,
He is Omnipresent."

May all people everywhere be happy
and prosperous; May all the world
have happiness and peace.

"When there is righteousness in the heart,
There is beauty in the character.
When there is beauty in the character,
There is harmony in the home.
When there is harmony in the home,
There is order in the nation.
When there is order in the nation,
There is peace in the world."

Have full faith in God and in yourselves. Engage always in good deeds, beneficial activities; speak always the truth, do not inflict pain by word or deed or even thought. That is the way to gain Santhi; that is the highest gain which you can earn in this life.

However high a bird may soar, it has sooner or later to perch on a tree top, to enjoy quiet. So too a
day will come when the most haughty, the most willful, the most unbelieving, even those who assert
that there is no joy or peace in the contemplation of the Highest Self, will have to pray:
"God, grant me peace, grant me consolation, strength and joy."

The advances in science and technology have enabled man to roam in the sky like birds and move in water like fish.
But he has not mastered the art of living well on the earth. If man has not learned how to lead a worthy human life,
what is the value of his existence? Make your life meaningful by doing your duty to your parents and your
Motherland. The man who is not proud of the land of his birth is worse than a corpse. Learn to love your country,
without any hatred for other countries. Get rid of differences based on community, creed or caste.
Regard all mankind as one family.

...Once **Krishna** *and* **Arjana** *were going together along the open road. Seeing a bird in the sky,* **Krishna** *asked* **Arjuna,** *"Is that a dove?"*

Arjuna *replied, "Yes, it is a dove."*

Krishna *then asked him, "Is it an eagle?"*

Arjuna *answered, "Yes, it is an eagle."*

"No, Arjuna, it looks like a crow to me. Is it not a crow?"

Arjuna *replied, "I'm sorry, it is a crow beyond a doubt."*

Krishna *laughed and chided him for his agreeing to whatever suggestion was given.*

But Arjuna said, "Forgive me; your words are far more weighty than the evidence of my eyes. You can make it a crow or a dove or an eagle; when you say it is a crow, it will be one." Implicit faith is the road to spiritual success.

For the bird in mid-ocean flying over the dark, deep waters, the only resting place is the mast of the ship sailing across. So too, the Lord is the only refuge for Man. However far the bird may fly, it knows where it can rest; that knowledge gives it confidence. It has the memory of the mast steady in its mind; its form is fixed in its eye. The Name of the Lord is the mast for you; remember it ever.

The heart represents the Atma. It is self-effulgent. The light from the heart (Atma) illumines the mind and enables it to see the eternal world. The mind is like the moon which receives its light from the sun. It has no light of its own.

Sadhana (spiritual practice) must render you calm, unruffled, poised, balanced. Make your mind cool and comfortable as moonlight, for the moon is the deity holding sway over the mind. Be calm in speech, be calm in response to malice, caviling and praise. Calmness of senses, passions, emotions, feelings, impulses— that is real **santhi** *(peace) ... Do not be led away by doubt and vain arguments; do not question how and whether I can do all this.*

Water running one direction in a stream reaches the sea; water which flows in several different directions is soaked up by the ground. Karmic impression (mental tracings) are like this. The holy stream of good **samskaras** (impressions) must flow full and steady along the fields of holy thoughts and finally abide in the great ocean of bliss at the moment of physical death. Worthy indeed is he who reaches such a goal!

Fish are happy because they are in water—when thrown out of the water they suffer mortal pain. Likewise, man is happy when he is immersed in Love, Peace and Truth; these are the components of the "water" that gives him life. When he is lacking the awareness of these, he suffers. The average life is like being thrown out of the water. Spiritual discipline is the struggle to leap back into the life-giving elements.

For a drowning man, even a stem of a plant is some support. So, to a person struggling in the Sea of **Samsara** (the flowing pattern of life), a few uplifting words may be of great help. No good deed can be wasted, and even bad deeds have their consequences. So, strive to avoid the slightest trace of negative activity; keep your eyes pure, fill your ears with the words of God and stories of Holy Deeds. Use the tongue to utter good words, useful and true. Such practice always reminds you of God and constant effort must grant you victory.

Peace is a shore-less ocean—it is the light that illuminates the world.

You must dive into the sea to get the pearls. What good does it do to dabble among the waves near the shore and assert that the sea has no pearls?

Transcendental Being is a shore-less, bottomless ocean. Swim about happily in this deep and undisturbed ocean; then only can one attain true peace.

I ask only for purity of heart to shower grace. Do not posit distance between you and me; do not interpose the formalities of the Guru-Sishya relationship, or even the attitude distinctions of the God-Devotee relationship between you and me. *I am neither Guru, nor God; I am You; You are I; that is the truth.* "I am Yours," "You are Mine," and finally "I am You." There is no distinction. That which appears so is the delusion. *You are waves; I am Ocean.* Know this and be free, be Divine.

On the vast ocean, countless waves are continually forming and disappearing. Each wave has its own form and shines in many colors. But none of them is separate from the ocean. Likewise, all the myriad beings in the world have their different names and forms but all are tiny droplets from the infinite ocean of *Sat-Chit-Ananda* (The Cosmic Being-Awareness-Bliss). All beings are manifestations of the Divine.

Like underground water, the Divine is there, in every one, remember. The Lord is Sarva-bhutaantaraathma, Sarvyapi. He is the Aathma of every being. He is in you as much as in every one else. He is not more in a rich being or bigger in a fat being; His spark illumines the cave of the heart of every one.

The waters of a river leap from mountains, fall into valleys and rush through gorges; besides, tributaries join at various stages and the water becomes turbid and unclean. So too, in the flood of human life, speed and power increase and decrease. These ups and downs might happen any moment during life. No one can escape these; they may come at the beginning of life or at the end or perhaps in the middle. *So, what man has to firmly convince himself is that life is necessarily full of ups and downs; and that far from being afraid and worried over these, he should welcome them as adding to his experience.* He should not only feel like this, but he should be happy and glad whatever happens to him. Then all troubles, whatever their nature, will pass away lightly and quickly. For this, the temper of the mind is essential.

The body is like a boat. Our life is like a river and we have to cross that river and reach our destination. Our destination is the destination of Divinity. Our life, the present one, is one of living in the contemporary world. In the process of our trying to cross the river of life and reach the destination of Divinity, the boat that we have to use, namely our body has to be safeguarded and taken great care of. This boat should not develop leakage en route.

Let us not find ourselves in the position illustrated by the plight of the reverent pastor of a church in the hill country. He had placed his life in God's care. A great storm broke over the hill country. Extraordinarily heavy rains fell on the hill and valley, the river rose high beyond all limits and the pastor's church was carried away in the flood. He found sanctuary for himself on the roof of his church. First, a man on the shore cried out that he would save the pastor by throwing a rope to him. The pastor's reply was, "No thanks. God is my Savior and God will save me." Then two men came in a boat with the same offer and received the same reply. Later on, just before the final disaster, some people in a motor launch approached with the intention of saving the pastor, but he again gave the same reply. After the final disaster, the pastor appeared at the pearly gates of heaven to seek admittance, and he complained to the guardian angels that God had deserted him in his hour of need. The angels, somewhat taken aback, replied, "But Pastor, we did send help to you. Right away we sent a man with a rope, and after that we sent two different boats!" In this same context, Baba once remarked, *"First there must be common sense, then comes Divine Sense."*

There is the story of a king, the minister and the servant going in a boat over a stormy lake. The servant was thrown into a panic, at the sight of water all round. There was danger of his upsetting the boat itself. So the minister caught hold of the fellow, pushed him into the water, dipped him a number of times in spite of his shrieks and then when he cried, "the boat, the boat," it was hoisted back. Once in the boat, he knew he was safe from the waters of which he was afraid. So too, we are in God, but yet afraid of the waters of **Samsara.** It is when we suffer the ordeals of Samsara that the security and safety of faith in God can be realized.

Born in water and momentarily floating on it, the water bubble disappears into the water. **Nara** (man), emerges from **Narayana** (God) and merges back into Him.

A bar of iron sinks in water, but beat it into a hollow vessel and it will float merrily and even carry some weight. **So too, man's mind sinks easily in the sea of senses; beat it hollow, hammering it with the Name of the Lord.** It will float, safely, on a sea of troubles. Do not be like gramophone records singing some one else's song, ignorant of the genuine thrill of music. Sing from your own experience the Glory and Grace of the Lord.

The ocean is vast, but a huge steamship is not needed to go on the ocean. Just a small tire will take one on the ocean.

We who are crossing the ocean of **Samsara** (the Chain of birth and death) need to cultivate the art of swimming through **Bhagavathchinthana** (Meditation on God). However learned we may be, if we do not have the training and cultivation, we are bound to sink. Life is a boat which enables us to cross the ocean of **Samsara** with the aid of meditation on God. **Vairagyam** or detachment does not imply renunciation of family ties and fleeing into the loneliness of the jungle. It means our giving up the feeling that things are permanent and capable of yielding supreme joy.

The Grace of God is as the ocean: vast, limitless.

The Atma is like the ocean; to instruct a person about it, you need not ask him to drink the entire ocean. A single drop placed on the tongue will give him the needed knowledge. So too, if you desire to know this **Upanishad**, the implication of one **Manthra**; you can realize the Goal without fail. Learn and practice. That is the secret of the teachings.

The mind is like a lake. When the water is calm, the rays of the sun are reflected on the surface of water, like a mirror. But if the water is disturbed because the wind is blowing, then there is very little reflection. Man must learn to control his mind.

There are some men who are like moths, who must bore through whatever they come across, silk or cotton or wool; there are others who are like bees, who seek only honey. The lotus attracts bees from afar, but the frogs that skip around it on the lake know naught of its beauty or fragrance.

Wisdom means the recognition of the immanence of the Divine in every being.

God is not involved in either rewards or punishments. He only reflects, resounds and re-acts! He is the Eternal Unaffected Witness! You decide your own fate. Even creation, protection and destruction follow the same law, the innate law of the maya-ridden universe.

First there is control of outer senses, then control of inner senses, then a sense of balance, with a limitation to freedom. Because, freedom is the end of wisdom. Then comes **pranayama** and **pratyahara**. **Brahma** is described as having the nature and wisdom. That is why it has been said that the end of wisdom is freedom. So, freedom means **Jnana Thatwa** or the light of wisdom, but not the unrestrained way in which we live our lives in this world.

Will power motivated by God is the active force available for your uplift. This is called **Sankalpa Bala**. Develop it by concentration and **japa**. The mind must be compelled to submit to the dictates of the will. Now, you are easily led astray, by the vagaries of the mind. *That is why, I say WATCH! W is for watch your Words; A is for watch your Actions; T is for watch your Thoughts; C is for watch your Character; H is for watch your Heart.* If the watch reminds you every second of the need to watch these five, you can be quite happy.

Embodiments of Divine Love! Consider for a moment wherefrom the rain comes.
It comes from clouds. The clouds have come from water vapor rising from the sea.
The rain becomes a channel on the earth, then a rivulet and then a big river which
joins the sea. A pot made out of clay, when it is broken, is cast on the ground,
where, in course of time, it becomes clay again. Water from the sea joins the sea,
clay from the earth goes back to earth again, man alone forgets the source from
which he came.

*What is the root cause of man's sorrow and sickness? Not being content with
what he has, and hankering after what he does not have, man forfeits
peace of mind.*

When it rains on sand, the water seeps down;
When it rains on red earth, the water stays;
When the rain falls on an oyster, a pearl is born;
Likewise, devotion grows according to one's worthiness.

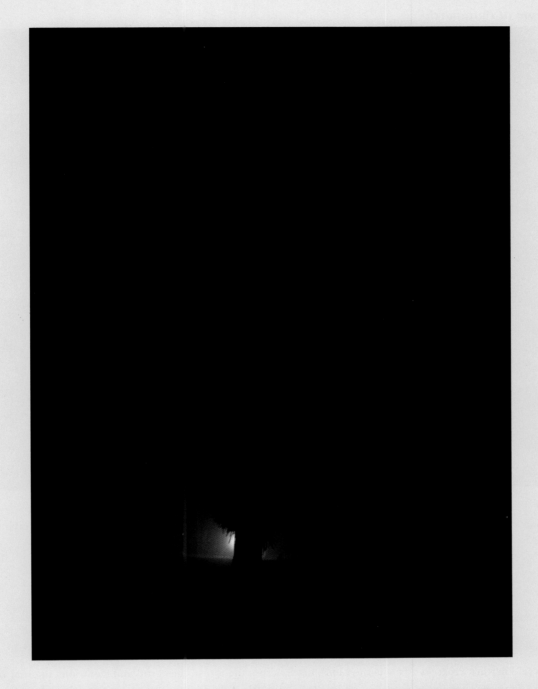

Practice silence. For the voice of God can be heard in the region of the heart only when the tongue is still ... *Silence is the speech of the spiritual seeker.* Soft sweet speech is the expression of genuine love. Hate screeches, fear squeals, conceit trumpets—but love sings lullabies; it soothes, it applies balm.

The best sadhana **is that every act through the day be done as worship of God. God is like electric power. The heart is the light bulb. The wiring is the discipline. The switch is the intelligence.**

The Museum at Puttaparthi

The wise man is he who keeps his reason sharp and clear, and sees things as they really are. He listens to the advice:

Life is a Challenge, Meet it;
Life is Love; Share it;
Life is a Dream; Realize it;
Life is a Game; Play it.

This is the real Pilgrim's Progress. This is the Lion's mark across the forest, masterful and victorious the roar of the lion makes all the denizens scamper in panic; so too the Halo of Wisdom scatters the dark brood of fear and doubt.

The Entrance of Prasanthi Nilayam—"The Ashram"

Puttaparthi

Only the man of faith is completely free from fear.

See good. Do good. Be good.

That is the way to God.

Where there is confidence, there is Love.

Where there is Love, there is Peace.

Where there is Peace, there is Truth.

Where there is Truth, there is Bliss.

Where there is Bliss, there is God.

The best Guru is the Divine in you;

yearn for hearing His Voice, His Upadesh.

Prayer must emanate from the heart,

where God resides, and not from the head where

doctrines and doubts clash.

Be happy that others are happy.

Patience is all the strength that man needs.

It is easy to conquer anger through love,

attachment through reasoning,

falsehood through charity.

People could not stand the Lord in super-human form. It is only when the Lord comes in human body that people are able to approach Him and learn to love Him and know Him even a little bit. But one should not make the mistake of thinking that is all there is to the Lord. For instance, the airplane flying high in the sky descends to the airport. But one should not make the mistake of thinking that the plane is a ground machine because they see it on the ground. Once it has taken on its load of passengers, it again zooms up high into the sky. In like fashion, although the Lord has made a landing here on earth, so to speak, He is not limited by His human form.

The person who serves is the person served. You serve yourself when you serve another.
You serve another because his suffering causes you anguish and by relieving it, you want to save yourself
from that anguish. *Unless you have the anguish, your service will be hollow and insincere.*

First you should look after yourself and not be a burden. That is the first thing. If you are not able to help so many people, it doesn't matter. But if you don't do anything that is harmful, that is real help. If you can't help a person, never mind. But don't harm anybody. To harm is bad.

The day when devotees hail the Lord with adoration;
The day when people fraternize with the poor and the distressed;
When the servants of the Lord are treated to a pleasing feast;
When the Great Ones come and relate the glories of the Lord;
That day alone is a sacred and memorable day;
All others are days of mourning.

So long as you live in the world, you have to conform to the rules and regulations governing the worldly affairs. But whatever you may do, you must not lose sight of the Supreme spiritual goal of life. You should recognize the fact that nothing belongs to you whether mother, father, brother, kinsman, wealth, house etc. All these ephemeral things are related to the changing body which is the basis for all mental aberrations.

The world will change only when the individual changes. When individuals are good, society also becomes good.
... it is only when man undergoes trials and tribulations, hardships, losses and sorrows that his real worth
will shine forth. A devotee should be ready to gladly accept anything as God's gift.

Through knowledge, you acquire humility. Through humility you become worthy of responsibility. Through wealth, you
must practice righteousness. Righteousness ensures your well-being in this world and the one beyond it ... Such persons
are fearless like lions. One who prays to God for something in return is like a wage-laborer.

Man's foremost duty is to make
The stream of Divine Love
Flow throughout the world.
It is not for living for himself
That every man has been born;
Only by having the noble thought
That he has to serve society
Will he ennoble himself
And achieve Self-satisfaction.

You may say that progress is possible only through My Grace, says Baba, but though My Heart is soft as butter, it melts only when there is some warmth in your prayer. Unless you make some disciplined effort, some Sadhana, Grace cannot descend on you. The yearning, the agony of unfulfilled aim, that is the warmth that melts My Heart. That is the anguish that wins Grace.

Among men, each one is himself the cause of his fortune, good or bad. He is himself the builder, the architect. Fate, destiny, pre-determination, the Will of God—everyone of these explanations is toppled by the principle of **Karma**. God and man can be reconciled and affiliated only on the basis of this **Sutra** or principle of **Karma**. When man realizes that God has no share in causing his suffering and that he is himself the sole cause, that no blame attaches to any other person, that he is the initiator as well as the beneficiary—the cause and the effect—of his acts, that he is free to shape his future, then he approaches God with a firmer step and a clearer mind.

Students should bear in mind the rules of right conduct that should govern their life. They are passing through the most precious and sacred period in their lives. This should be well used. Dedicate all your thoughts and aspirations to God and surrender yourselves to the Will of the Divine. Surrender may appear to be difficult, but it is not so. It is, in fact, like keeping your money in the bank. You will be able to draw money from the bank when ever you need it. Similarly when you have entrusted all your concerns to **Bhagavan**, you can draw from Him whatever you need. What is it that stands in the way of this surrender? It is your ego and your possessiveness. You do not have sufficient trust in the Lord. People desperately cling to their possessions saying: "My money, my house" and so on. They forget that when you surrender to the Divine, you acquire His Grace. Some time or other your wealth will go. But once you have earned the Grace of God, you can feel secure and satisfied. Bhagavan does not need your wealth. He is always a *Chittachora* (one who steals the heart), not a *Vithachoras*, (stealer of wealth). It is you who have to change from *Vithachoras*, to *Chithachora*.

Moderation in life is necessary, otherwise there is no reserve of energy. Food must be in the body for
some time for the benefit of the energy reserve. Too much exercise uses up the food energy before it can
be added to the reserve. So there is no gain. Likewise, the human system cannot withstand too much talking.

If you desire to cultivate one-pointedness, do not, when in a crowd or bazaar, scatter your vision to the
four corners and on everything, but see only the road in front of you, just enough to avoid accidents to yourself.
One-pointedness will become firmer if one moves about without taking one's attention off the road,
avoiding dangers, and not casting eyes on others' forms.

Gold necklace with precious stone materialized by Sai Baba
out of His hand for one of His devotees at her wedding

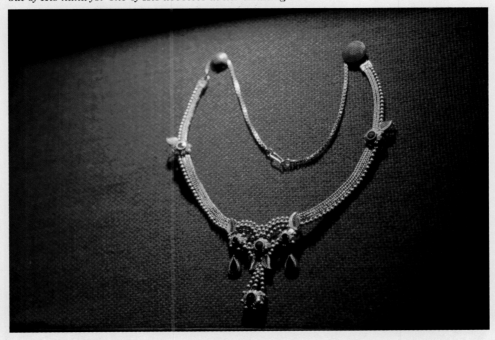

In the world, the metal, the stone, the jeweler are all separate, as is the one who will take the ring. But they must be brought together. Whereas, in the world of Swami, the metal, the stone, the jeweler and the one who will take the ring are all one, and that One is God. In the world, time is needed. But God is beyond time. Immediately the ring is ready.

The formula that nothing can be created out of nothing is appropriate to the limited field and dimensions of science. It does not at all apply to the transcendental field and dimensions of spirituality. In the latter field, anything can be created by the supreme will. All that exists can be made to disappear and what does not exist can be made to appear.

Our history and tradition, scripture as well as literature, are full of such incidents which they call miracles. The material laws and formulas simply do not apply to Divinity. For me, this is not a matter of any mystery or mystique. What I will, happens: what I order, materializes.

Spiritual and moral values have to be honored as much as,
if not more than, economic and material values.

Where money is calculated and garnered, and exhibited to
demonstrate one's achievements, I will not be present.
I come only where sincerity, faith and surrender are valued.

There are a number of pots made of clay, wood, copper, brass, silver and gold. They are filled with water. The reflections of the sun can be seen in the water in all the pots. Is it possible to say that the reflection of the sun in one pot is good and that in another is bad? The value of the pots may vary. But can any value be given to the sun's reflection in each of them? The pots are products of nature. The sun is transcendental. The pot can vary in quality. But the sun is incomparably pure. He symbolises the Infinite Spirit. Every living being is an image of the Supreme. Without a vessel, water cannot be contained. Without water the sun's image cannot be seen. In a human being, the mind represents water. The body is the container (vessel), the Spirit (Atma) that dwells in the body corresponds to the reflection of the sun.

Allow the wind of doubt or the sun of despair to affect the pot of **Ananda** you have filled, and it will evaporate quickly. But keep the pot in the water of good company and good deeds; it can be preserved undiminished for ever. Ananda too grows when you dwell on it in silence and recapitulate the circumstances which yielded it.

Whatever talent a person has, should be dedicated to the service of the rest of humanity, indeed, of all living beings. Therein lies fulfillment.

Dedicate your talents to the service of all beings.

Make your life a rose that speaks silently in the language of fragrance.

Offer your talents at the feet of God; let everyone be a flower, free from
creeping worms of envy and egoism, and full of the fragrance.

The nature of the mind is to be occupied. Even when still, like the feathers on a peacock, there is a shimmering, an apparent movement in the mind. Like the Aspen tree, even on a still morning its leaves seem to tremble and move. It is the nature of the mind to dwell upon things. So, the proper method to deal with the mind is to direct the mind's activity towards good deeds, good thoughts, repetition of the Name of the Lord, and not allow it to be aimed at harmful objects, harmful thoughts and deeds.

The heart is like a field. It has to be cultivated properly. It should be filled with the water of love. It should be tilled by the process of enquiry *(vichara)*. Then the seed of the Divine Name has to be planted in it. You must erect the fence of vigilance to guard it. You must protect the crop (of devotion) by weeding out egoism. Only then you will reap the fruit of love for the Divine.

…my objective is the establishment of **Sanathana Dharma** which believes in one God as propitiated by the founders of all religions. So no one has to give up his religion or deity, but through them worship the one God in all. I have come not to disturb or destroy, but to confirm and vindicate everyone in his own faith.

In the Garden of the Heart, the fifth flower is **Shanti** (Inner Peace). Shanti does not mean that a person should not react at all, whatever others may say or however they may abuse them. It does not mean that he must be silent as a rock. It involves mastery of all the senses and all the passions. Inner peace must become one's nature. Shanti has detachment as the basic quality. The sea which likes to gather and possess, lies low; the cloud that likes to renounce and give is high up in the sky. Shanti endows man with unruffled mind and steady vision. The prayer for Shanti is usually repeated thrice. "OM, Shanti, Shanti, Shanti," since peace is prayed for in the physical, mental and spiritual planes.

You should adore the same Lord whom you worship. That is My image. I am present in That form also.
That form is also Mine. Worship offered to Him also reached Me.

Those attached to God, aspiring for God, aware of God,
have certain distinct marks by which they can be identified.
Pronouncing judgments like this quite contrary to the nature of dedication.
Again such people have a compassionate heart.
If a person turns the rosary on the fingers, and is intently
engaged in watching the tip of his nose, unmindful of the distress
that dances around him, we can best name him a sloth, that is all.
Get up, place the rosary in its bag, and engage yourselves
in relieving distress--that is the true spiritual path.
Do not waste all your years with stone images, pictures or idols.
Learn to see in every living vital active person, the embodiment of all energy,
all beauty, all beneficence, namely, God. God is subtler
than ether, filling the smallest crevice with His Majesty.
Know this and serve His manifestations, wherever you meet them…

Continue to worship your chosen God along lines already famil-
iar to you. There is no need to change your chosen God and
adopt a new one when you have seen Me and heard Me.

Scriptures of different religions appear different but their aim is
the same, to establish the brotherhood of man and Fatherhood
of God as the basis for peace for mankind.

Let the different faiths exist, let them flourish, let the Glory of God be sung in all the languages and in a variety
of tunes; that should be the ideal. Respect the differences between the faiths and recognize them as valid
as far as they do no extinguish the flame of unity.

See in Me yourself...
For I see Myself in all of you...

You are My Life, My Breath, My Soul...
You are all My Forms.
When I love you, I love Myself...
When you love yourself, you love Me...

I separated Myself from Myself so that I may be Myself...
I separated Myself from Myself and became All of this
So that I may be Myself.

Reason can be tamed only by discipline.

Concentration means when all senses and desires fall away and there is only God. The concentration of **Ramakrishna Paramahamsa** was naturally so strong that he grew something of a tail when meditating on **Hanuman**, the monkey. His body was just a changing bubble, his concentration was so strong. Special work on concentration need not be a part of meditation. Concentration is already in force wherever mind, intelligence and senses are used.

To diminish the wanderings of your thoughts, repeat the Name of the Lord; that will keep out your sorrows and troubles.

In our country, there is a peculiar method of trapping monkeys. This process consists of bringing a big pot with a small mouth and keeping some material which is attractive to the monkey inside the pot. The monkey will put its hand inside the pot and catch hold of a handful of the material. It will then not be able to pull out its hand from within the pot. It will imagine that someone inside the pot is holding its hand. Then it makes an attempt to run away along with the pot, but the monkey is thus trapped. No one is holding the monkey. The monkey has trapped itself, because it has taken in its hand such a lot of material. The moment it lets the material in its hand go, it will be free.

In the same manner, in this big pot of the world with the narrow mouth of the family, man is tempted by the pleasures of the world, and when he gets lost with involvement in these pleasures he thinks that someone or something is binding him down. No other person is responsible for this bondage. The moment he gives up the pleasures and detaches himself, he will be free. That is the way to free himself from the imagined bondage.

"You are I."

"Give up the idea that you are the doer and that you are the beneficiary.
You can do this by dedicating both deed and fruit to the Lord.

Then no sin can affect you, for you are not the doer and the deed must perforce be holy."

Liberation comes through intellectual awareness of the Unity that underlies the Diversity. Have no thorn of hate in your mind, develop love towards all. Desire is a storm, greed is a whirlpool, pride is a precipice, attachment is an avalanche, egoism is a volcano. Keep these things away so that when you recite the Name of God or do meditation, they do not disturb the equanimity. Let love be enthroned in your heart. Then, there will be sunshine and cool breezes and gurgling waters of contentment feeding the roots of faith.

Total renunciation and karma yoga both lead you to the same goal of liberation. There is greater joy in doing work than in giving up work. Renunciation and work are not contradictory; they go together.

Twenty hammer-strokes might not succeed in breaking a stone; the twenty-first stroke might break it.
But, does this mean that the twenty blows were of no avail? No. Each of those twenty strokes
contributed its share to the final success. Likewise, the mind is engaged in a struggle with
the world, both internal and external. Needless to say, success might not always be your lot, but man can
attain everlasting bliss by immersing himself in good works and by saturating the mind with the love of God.
Infuse every moment of life with that love.

You have to busy yourselves with activity in order to use time and skill to the best advantage. The dull and the ignorant will hesitate to be active for fear of exhaustion or failure or loss. The emotional and passionate individuals will plunge headlong and rare for quick results and will be disappointed if they do not come in. The balanced persons will be active because it is their duty; they will not be agitated by anything--failure or success. The Godly will take up activity as a means of worshipping God and they leave the results to God. They know that they are but instruments of God.

Man is made to work hard, and if one is working hard in service to the Lord in one way or the other, the mind will not have time to be occupied with useless, random thoughts. And if there is no outside work, then the work of spiritual endeavor should go on, in the way of meditation, recitation of the Name, reading good books, talking with good people, and so on.

Karma is like the trail of dust behind the moving carriage. When the carriage stops, the dust will settle on it.
But the carriage cannot forever continue fast along the road in order to escape the dust.
The best course is to get on the paved highway, away from the dust-track. That is to say,
man must acquire the Grace of God and move along the path smoothed by it.

Carry only one load, the desire to win Grace.

Difficulties are created to increase the "yearning" and to lift
the sincere devotee from the rest.

In western countries now, God is denied, and man is relying on himself. He exaggerates his own intelligence and sense of adventure and prides himself on the advance he has made through science and technology. But, intelligence without equanimity is filling mental hospitals. Peace is fleeing from the hearts of men and women; social harmony is becoming a distant dream, international concord is a mirage pursued by a few. Man travels to the moon, but does not explore his own inner levels of consciousness, and understanding them, cleanse them and control them.

In western countries now, God is denied, and man is relying on himself. He exaggerates his own intelligence and sense of adventure and prides himself on the advance he has made through science and technology. But, intelligence without equanimity is filling mental hospitals. Peace is fleeing from the hearts of men and women; social harmony is becoming a distant dream, international concord is a mirage pursued by a few. Man travels to the moon, but does not explore his own inner levels of consciousness, and understanding them, cleanse them and control them.

The **Kathopanishad** has compared the senses to horses. What are the characteristics of a horse? It can run fast. But once a bridle is put in its mouth, its entire movement can be controlled. How is it that a small bridle is able to control such a large animal? For the horse the mouth is the most important. In the human context the mouth is the most important among the five sense organs. With a small flame we can kindle a big fire. The power of speech is like the flame. With its fire we can do many things. By controlling the tongue you can acquire the capacity to master the world. Using the power of speech (**Vaak**) you can achieve something splendid or indulge in something mean. Speech can be employed for blessing one or blaming one. In a dithyramb in praise of the tongue, **Jayadeva** sings: "Oh tongue! You are pure! You are sweet! Do not indulge in idle talk. Sing the glories of the **Lord-Govinda! Damodara! Madhava!**"

Dhaynayoga is possible only on the basis of this **Nishkaama-karma**. If the mind is not under control and amenable to one's orders, it can become one's greatest foe. So live in solitude so that you can master the senses. A horse without reins, a bull unused to the yoke and a Sadhaka whose senses are not mastered are like a river without water. Such Sadhana is a waste.

There is no use resisting or fighting thoughts. If suppressed, they are always ready to spring forth at weak moments-like snakes in a basket. If the cover gets loose or is removed, the snakes spring forth. The way to overcome bad thoughts and impulses is by having thoughts of serving the Lord, good conversations with wise people, good actions and words. The weight of good acts and thoughts will bury the seeds of bad actions and thoughts. Both good and bad thoughts and impulses are like seeds in the mind. If buried too deeply in the earth, seeds rot and waste away. Good thoughts and deeds bury bad seeds so deeply that they rot and pass away and are no longer ready to spring forth.

While proceeding along the road, you can watch your shadow falling on mud or dirt, hollow or mound, thorns or sand, wet or dry patches of land. The shadow and its experiences are not **Nithyam** or **Sathyam**. Similarly, you must get convinced that `you' are but the shadow of the **Paramatma** and you are essentially not this `You' but **Paramatma** itself. That is the remedy for sorrow, travail and pain. Of course, it is only at the end of a long and systematic process of Sadhana that you will get fixed in the truth; until then, you are apt to identify yourself with this body and forget that the body which casts a shadow is itself a shadow.

When the tender plant of devotion begins to grow, it must be protected. When a
young tree is growing, various animals will eat it and may kill it. For this reason
a fence is placed around the young tree to protect it. When the tree is grown
it needs no protection. The same animals who would have first destroyed it,
now seek and find shade and shelter beneath its branches.

The Lord is the primordial seed. The Cosmos is the gigantic tree that has come from Him. In this tree, every country or nation is like a branch. Human beings are the fruits in the tree.

No tree will yield fruits the moment you plant the seedling in your backyard. To reach that stage, you have to follow carefully without break, the preparatory disciplines. No one can acquire the fruit without vigilance and steadfastness.

A single mango seed is planted; the tree yields thousands of fruits and in every fruit, you find the seed! The same **Aathma** is in every Being! *The Lord is the seed that is manifested as thousands of seeds.*

God is a "divine wish-fulfilling tree" that gives you whatever you ask for. But, you have to go near the tree and wish for the thing you want. The atheist is a person who is far away from the tree; the believer in God is one who is near to the tree-that is the difference. The tree does not make any distinction; it grants boons to all. God will not punish or take revenge if you do not recognize Him. He has no special form of worship which can please Him.

The truth is that life is like a tree where the various mental vicars of passions like Anger, Greed, Hate, Jealousy are the birds infesting and contaminating our hearts and robbing us of our Peace and Joy. Chant the Divine Names with love and rhythm, "Rama, Krishna, Govinda, Narayana." These birds of evil vicars infecting our minds and plaguing our lives will get a fright and fly away. Hearing even the names of ordinary, material things like "Fire!", "Snake!", or "Lemonade!" causes strong reactions in our minds. How much more strong and subtle would be the effect of uttering or hearing the Name of **Sarveswara**, who is the Creator and the Supreme Lord of the Universe?

Just as from a seed a tree can come, with innumerable branches, flowers and fruits, with a seed in each fruit, from the single seed to the Divine the infinite variety of Nature (**Prakriti**) has emerged. The relations between beings in the cosmos can be compared to the relations between the branches in a tree. Our feelings may be compared to flowers and life itself may be compared to the fruit. In each being, there is a seed of the Divine.

We have to learn good things from others. We sow seeds in the ground. We provide it with soil, manure and water. The seed sprouts, becomes a sapling and grows into a huge tree. It does not become soil when placed therein, nor manure when it feeds thereon, nor water when it partakes thereof. It only imbibes from each of them whatever it can benefit from them. It grows into what is essentially IT, namely, a huge tree!

A man borrowed money from another and promised to return it at sunrise the next day. The other fellow asked, "But, how are you certain that the sun will rise tomorrow?" At this, the creditor retorted, "But, how are you certain that I will live to repay it or that you will live to take it back?" Everything about life is uncertain. So, march on, from this very moment, take at least a few steps towards the goal, while you can. That very attempt might induce the Lord to extend your stay until you attain the goal.

The cow eats grass and drinks gruel, but out of these it creates sweet sustaining milk; so too, let the experiences which are gathered by your senses help in the production of the sweetness of kindness, the purity of devotion and the sustenance of santhi.

Regard the heart as a vast field. Use the mind as a plough. Treat the qualities (**gunas**) as bullocks. Use the intelligence (**viveka**) as a whip. With these aids, cultivate the field of your heart. What is the crop that is to be grown in it? Truth, Right Conduct, Peace, and Love. Devotion (**Bhakti**) is the rain, mediation (**Dhyana**) is the manure. Bliss (**Brahmananda**) is the crop. This is your task today. Cultivate the heart to raise a harvest of Truth, Right Conduct, Peace and Love. This crop has to be raised in your heart and should be shared with others.

People ask, "Where is God?' The answer is provided by Nature. Who is it that has created the five elements, the five life-breaths, the five sheaths, the five external sense organs and the five internal sense organs, which are all ceaselessly carrying out their functions according to their prescribed roles? The seasons in their regular cycle are teaching a lesson to man. Therefore, Nature is the demonstrable proof for the existence of God. Nature is not under any obligation to any man, it takes no orders from any man, it operates according to the Will of the Divine.

There is no need to retire into a forest or cave to know your inner Truth and to conquer your lower nature. As a matter of fact, you have no chance to exhibit your anger there and so victory achieved there may not be lasting or genuine. Win the battle of life, being in the world but yet, away from its tentacles.
That is the victory for which you deserve congratulations.

Stillness and Silence mean the nature of Pure Consciousness.
He who has reached it will be in the highest peace and highest bliss.

Pure Consciousness is Truth, Wisdom and Bliss.

Everyone has to be asked to approach Me and experience Me.
In order to get an idea of a mountain, it is not enough if you show a stone and say, "The mountain is a million times the size of this."
You will have to see an actual mountain, at least from a distance.

When man taps the energy of the Divine in himself, he can
easily master Nature, which is only the
vestige of the Divine. Through Truth, you can experience
Love; through love, you can visualize Truth.
Love God and you see God in every creature.

But going to many **gurus** is like a man who owns an acre. He
digs a bit here, then moves over to a new spot and
digs a little, and so on. Finally, he digs one hole five feet deep
and finds water. The total of all his diggings was perhaps 30
feet. At last, in one digging, he did find water, but his acre
was spoiled by the many shallow holes dug here and there.
Had he stayed with one hole and dug 30 feet, he would have
found his water. The acre is the spiritual heart.
All the holes are different gurus. Now the spiritual heart is
ruined by so many holes; they are leaks.

When you scatter seeds on the surface of the soil, they do not germinate. You have to keep them inside the soil. So too, Bodha, if it is scattered on the surface, will not germinate, grow into the tree of knowledge and yield the fruit of wisdom. Plant it in the heart, water the plant with Prema, manure it with Faith and Courage, keep off pests with the insecticides of Bhajana and Sathsanga, so that you can benefit in the end. You have not yet got started in Sadhana; still you demand Santhi; you demand Grace. How is it ever possible? Start! Then, everything will be added unto you.

Offerings that are made with no defilement of egoism are gladly accepted by the Lord. If you feel proud or conceited, even the most fragrant flowers placed at the Feet of the Lord will be rejected by Him as unbearably stinking.

The land need not be tilled or fenced in, no manuring or irrigation need be done if you are bent on growing only grass. It is only when you are eager to reap a harvest of edible grain that the sadhana of ploughing, watering, manuring and fencing are important. See God installed in everyone, and every living body as a temple where the Omnipresent God is to be adored and worshipped by your **seva**. You proclaim that God is resident in all creatures, but when you have to put that into action, your faith disappears and you discover excuses.

Ananda or bliss is the one and only achievement
for which life is to be devoted .... You cannot have
Ananda (**Bliss**) before faith.

Pure love can emanate only from a heart
immersed in peace.

Puttaparthi in the morning

...in the evening

A half hour in the morning and a half hour in the evening is enough for sitting
meditation. Spiritual practice should be varied for interest. Just as in daily life,
some variety makes the day interesting.

Prashaanthi Nilayam University at Puttaparthi

The morning shadow moves in front of you. However fast you run, you cannot catch it, on plain or mountain. Or, the shadow may pursue you and you cannot escape from it. This is the nature of desire. You may pursue it or it may pursue you--but you cannot overcome it or catch it. Desire is an insubstantial shadow. But turn desire inward, towards spiritual treasure, then it yields substantial results.

Surrender the ego, dedicate every moment and every movement to Him. He has assured mankind that He will ensure liberation from pain and evil. When asked where God is, people point towards the sky or some far distant region; that is why He is not manifesting Himself. Realize that He is in you, with you, behind you, before you and all around you; and He is all mercy, eager and anxious to fulfill your prayers, if they arise from a pure heart.

Where there is Faith there is Love
Where there is Love there is Peace
Where there is Peace there is Truth
Where there is Truth there is Bliss
Where there is Bliss there is God.

The cosmos, which includes the stars, the sun, and the earth, is but a flake of froth on the surface of the Atma, or universal soul. The consciousness that cognizes is only a wave on that sea. The sea itself is the **Atma, or universal soul consciousness.** The Atma alone is real; the rest is all appearance. The play of name and form, both are temporary and transient.

The **Atma** alone is the source of inner strength, it is the fountain spring of Joy, unaffected by reverses or victories.

The **Atma** is every one, vast and expansive. We fancy that the Atma is in us, in each of us.

God is only one. Your forms of worship, rituals and beliefs are purely personal and do not relate to the universal. "Divinity" means "that which is whole, all-embracing." The one Divine is present in all beings. Every being is filled with Truth and Love. There is no one without love. The love may find outlets in different ways, but it is essentially one. That love is God. Do not go against that Love.

In a river, the water is flowing in a swift current. But even tiny fish are able to swim in it and move about merrily. In the same river, a huge elephant, caught in the rapids, is likely to get washed away or drowned in spite of its enormous size. Whatever the speed of the current, the small fish are able to swim freely in the river and enjoy themselves. But an elephant is unable to survive in it. The reason is: What you need for survival in a river is not bulk, but the ability to swim.

Likewise, man who is caught up in the ocean of worldly existence (*Samsaara*) needs, not so much metaphysics, scholarship, or detachment, as the grace of Divine Love. Without any knowledge of *Vedanta*, if one is blessed with God's love, he can surmount all problems of life. Without faith in God, all scholarship, wealth or name and fame are of no avail.

What need is there for you to feel separateness between I and You? When you travel in a carriage, do you take the carriage as `I'? Look at the Sun. He gets reflected in a small pot filled with water, in a broad river, in a mirror, or on a polished pot. For this reason does the Sun feel that all these things are `He'? Does He get sad when the pot breaks, or the river gets dry? This is exactly like that. If you take `I' to be the body, then it is all bother! If you don't take it so, you will shine like the Sun, independent of anything else. Besides, You will be immanent everywhere.

No one yet knows the mystery of the electric current, why it behaves so, what is the exact nature of its origin and flow; but, yet it is manipulated into a thousand uses and it is manifesting through a thousand appliances and instruments. So too, God is present everywhere; but we can understand only that part of Him that manifests before our cognition. Ordinary people will swear that the earth does not move at all; it is held forth in poetry as a symbol of stability. But, it has two motions, both unbelievably fast! It rotates on its own axis at a speed which exceeds a thousand miles per hour; even while rotating so, the earth moves round the Sun at an astonishing rate of speed! But, do we notice it while it happens? God too is a reality, ever present in us and in every being; but we miss Him as we miss the movement of the earth.

Travel light even in the journey of life.

You are in the light; the Light is in you; You are the Light.

Life is a journey from the position I to the position WE,
from the singular to the plural, from the imprisoned One to the liberated One,
who is seen in the Many. The vision of the One, immanent in the obvious Many is the
fulfillment of all the years of one's life. This is the teaching contained
in the ancient texts and scriptures.

Man is a pilgrim set on a long journey; he has started from the stone, moved on to the vegetable and animal, and has now come to the human stage. He has still a long way to go, to reach the Divine, and so, he should not tarry. Every moment is precious; every step must take him further and nearer.

You have only a few years of life remaining. Why take the risks? Start early, drive carefully, arrive safely.

Remember death. The body is the car in which you are riding to death. You may meet death any moment while riding. Some tree or lorry, culvert or slush will bring it about. If you remember that time is running out every moment, you will not be tempted to waste time in idle talk or vain pursuits, wanton mischief or vulgar entertainment. Travel in the car carefully, slowly and with due regard for the needs of others on the road. Do not greedily try to overtake others or compete in speed.

The secret of liberation lies not in the mystic formula that is whispered in the ear and rotated on the rosary. It lies in the stepping out into action, walking forward in practice, the pious pilgrim route and the triumphant reaching of the goal.

Everything that is not "you" is an object; it is luggage for the journey; the less of it, the more comfortable the journey!

You may ask, "Who is God?" Ask and receive the answer to another question, "who am I?" This chance you have of a life-time of mental and physical activity is a letter encased in an envelope which you have to drop into the red box, called Nature (the Universe, Creation). You have to write there your real address, and where it has to go, which destiny this life has to attain. About life, the two fundamental questions are: From? To? And, for both, you have not discovered the answer, though you have grown to be pretty quick in asking a thousand other irrelevant questions!

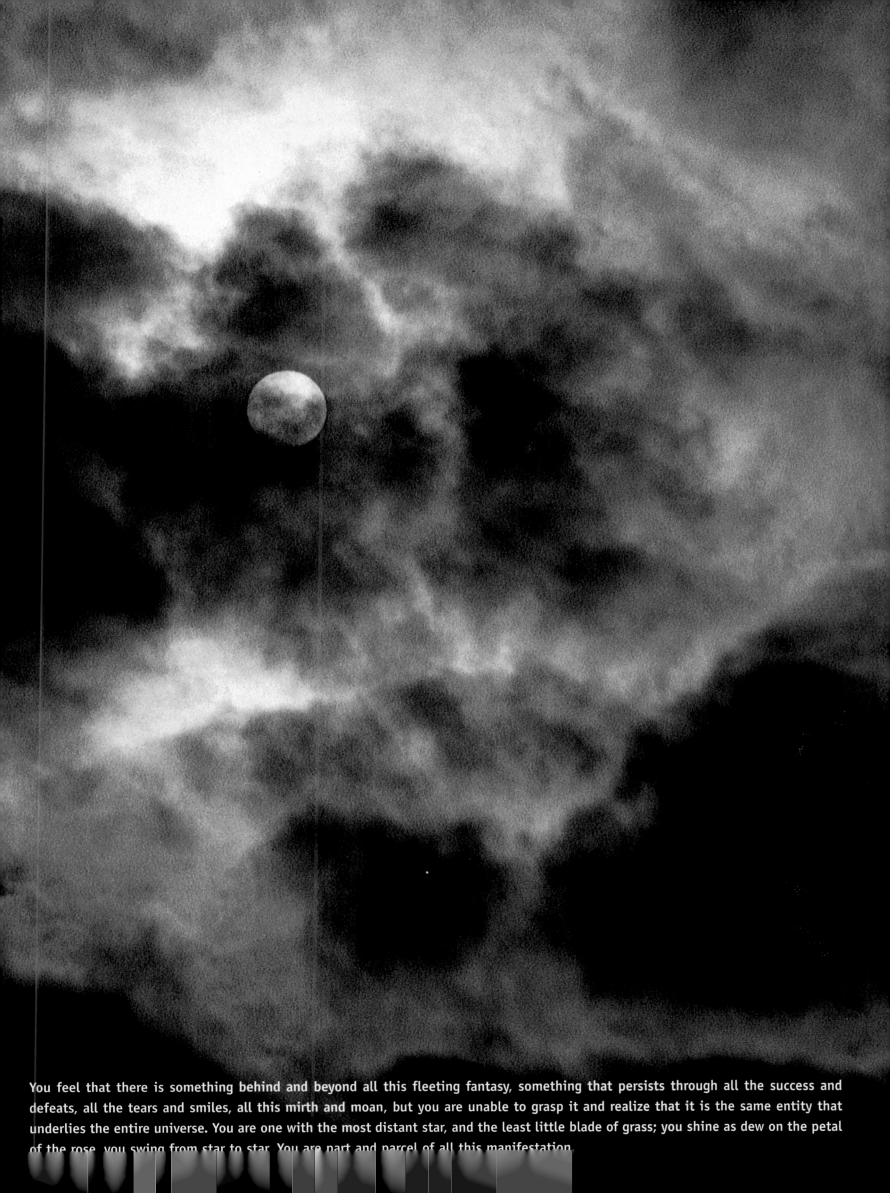

You feel that there is something behind and beyond all this fleeting fantasy, something that persists through all the success and defeats, all the tears and smiles, all this mirth and moan, but you are unable to grasp it and realize that it is the same entity that underlies the entire universe. You are one with the most distant star, and the least little blade of grass; you shine as dew on the petal of the rose, you swing from star to star. You are part and parcel of all this manifestation.

God dwells in you as Joy. That is why you seek Joy always in every object around you. To become as full of Joy as **Radha** or **Ramakrishna** or **Vivekananda**, you have to sacrifice your ego, and saturate yourself with the Lord, with the consciousness that the Lord is your being. So long as you have a trace of ego in you, you cannot see the Lord clearly. Egoism will be destroyed if you constantly tell yourself, "It is He not I." "He is the force, I am but the instrument." Keep His name always on the tongue. Contemplate His glory whenever you see or hear anything beautiful or grand; see in everyone the Lord, Himself, moving in that form. Welcome every chance to help others, to console them, to encourage them along the spiritual path.

Heart must understand heart, heart must be drawn to heart, if friendship must last. Friendship must bind two hearts and affect both of them beneficially, whatever may happen to either --loss or gain, pain or pleasure, good fortune or bad. The bond must survive all the blows of fate and be unaffected by time, place and circumstances. Each must correct the other; and each must welcome criticism and comment from the other; for each knows that they come from sympathy and love. Each must be vigilant that the other does not slide from the ideal, cultivate habits that are deleterious, or hide thoughts and plans that are productive of evil. The honor of each is in the safe keeping of the other. Each trusts the other and places reliance on their other's watchful love. Only those deserve the name--friends who help in uplifting life, cleansing ideals, elevating emotions and strengthening resolve.

On the electric current, the positive and the negative together produce light.
The positive pole is Grace, Divine Majesty, basking in His Glory. The negative pole
is the consciousness `Not I' `Not Mine'; the denial of the deluding experiences of
the waking, the dream and the deep-sleep stages, the destruction of the warp
and woof of the mind, the process of weeding and cleansing.

Seek the company of good men even at the sacrifice of your honor and life. But, be praying to God to bless you with the discrimination needed to distinguish between good men and those lacking the virtues. You must use the intellectual powers given to you.

When you get violent and angry with any one, quietly go and drink a glass of
cold water or repeat the name of the Lord to overcome it, or spread your bed
and lie down until the fit of fury passes. While angry, you abuse another and he
does the same; and tempers rise, heat is generated and lasting injury is done.
Five minutes of anger damages the relationship for five generations.

All mankind must be welcomed into the warm fold of your love.
Seek the good in others and the evil in yourself.

The tongue guards the human heart. An atom bomb will destroy the body,
but the tongue is a weapon that can destroy the heart of man.

Instead of searching for others' faults, search for your own faults yourself; uproot them,
throw them off. It is enough if you search and discover one fault of yours; that is better
than discovering tens of hundreds of faults in others.

"Oh man, it is because you lack love and are filled with selfishness that the world is plunged in so much conflict and chaos. It is only when you develop love and the spirit of sacrifice that you will realize the divinity that is in the human."

There are four things in which every man must interest himself: who am I, where from have I come, whither am I going, how long shall I be here.

It is your duty to ask God. Words must be said and the words must correspond to the thought. The thought must be put into a true word. It is true enough that the Divinity knows all. But He requires that the true word be said. The mother may know that to maintain life the child requires food. But milk is given when the child asks for it.

Even when you have to speak harshly to a child or a parent because all other means of bringing a point home have failed, let your heart be soft, let it not be hardened by prejudices or hatred ... the basis of the teacher's **Sadhana** is love.

The root is education and the fruit is virtue.

Children are the crops growing in the fields to field the harvest on which the nation has to sustain itself.
Children are like realized souls without attachment.
In children, the mind is in its native purity; for, they have no sense of mine.

Love is God; God is Love;
where there is Love,
there God is evident.

Love more and more people, love them more and more intensely.
Transform the love into service. Transform the service into
worship. That is the highest **Sadhana**.

Brightness in the face, splendor in the eye, a determined look, a noble gaze, pleasant voice, open-hearted charity, unwavering goodness: these are the signs of a progressing will to attain the vision of God.

God's eye does not see purity or impurity. It is all in your vision only. As you think, so you become.

I want each of you to grow into a strong, steady and straight person. Your eyes should not seek evil sights; your tongue should not seek evil speech; your hands should not seek evil acts; your minds should not seek evil thoughts. Be pure and be full of Love. Help those who are in a worse condition and serve those who need your help.

Human values cannot be practiced by studying books or listening to lectures. They have to be cultivated by individual efforts.

Education can yield peace and prosperity only when, along with technical skills and objective information, students are equipped with moral ideas, righteous living and spiritual insight … Spiritual education is not a separate and distinct discipline; it is part and parcel of all types and level of education.

It is only when there is a close relationship of selfless love between the teacher and the student and right education is imparted from the heart that knowledge will blossom into wisdom … the teacher dedicates himself to a great spiritual discipline when he enters this profession. He himself has to be what he advises the pupils to be. The tender minds in the classroom are easily molded by his example.

Students have to cultivate gratitude, compassion and tolerance. Sympathy with the distressed is a fundamental human quality ... It is the young who need guidance for they should avoid the bad precedents set by elders and pursue the path of truth, honesty and hard work ...

Those who seek to impart values must first practice them themselves and set an example ... You can teach Love to students only through Love ... The teacher has the greatest role in molding the future of the country. Of all professions, his is the noblest, the most difficult and the most important. He should be an example to his pupils. If a teacher has a vice, thousands are polluted. If he is dedicated and pure, thousands of children will be improved and the nation will gain from educated men and women of character.

The end of knowledge is wisdom,
the end of culture is perfection,
the end of wisdom is freedom,
the end of education is character.

Love as thought is Truth.

Love as action is Right Conduct.

Love as feeling is Peace.

Love as understanding is Non-violence.

The age span 16-30 is crucial, for that is the period when life adds sweetness to itself, when talents, skills, and attitudes are accumulated, sublimated and sanctified. If the tonic of unselfish Seva is administered to the mind during this period, life's mission is fulfilled – for the process of sublimation and sanctification will be hastened by this tonic. Do not serve for the sake of reward, attracting attention, or earning gratitude, or from a sense of pride at your own superiority in skill, wealth, status, or authority. Serve because you are urged by love. When you succeed, ascribe the success to the Grace of God, who urged you on, as Love within you. When you fail, ascribe the failure to your own inadequacy, insincerity or ignorance.

A span of life allotted to man is very short; the World in which he lives is very wide; time extends far behind and far beyond. What little man has to do here has to be done quickly, at the place that is assigned to him and within the time that is allotted to him. And, man has such a formidable task before him; it is to fulfill it that he has come as man, exchanging for this human habitat all the merit he has acquired during many past lives. The task is no less than the manifestation of the Divinity latent in man.

The mother is the pillar of the home, society, nation and of humanity itself. Mothers must know the secret of mental peace, of inner silence, of spiritual courage, of contentment (which is the greatest wealth) and of spiritual discipline which give lasting joy.

If you want to know how advanced a nation is, study the mothers: are they free from fear and anxiety, are they full of Love towards all, are they trained in fortitude and virtue? If you like to imbibe the glory of a culture, watch the mothers, rocking the cradles, feeding, fostering, teaching, and fondling the babies.

Love for the mother has to be fostered by everyone. Whoever she may be, a mother is verily divine. She is indeed the first teacher for everyone. It is only the mother who strives most for securing the well-being of the child by showering on him boundless affection and love and shoeing him the father.

The child has its tongue and the mother has hers. The mother keeps the child on her lap and pronounces the words so that the child may learn to speak. However busy the mother's tongue may be, the child has to speak through his own tongue. The mother cannot speak for the child and save herself all the bother! The Guru, too, is like that. He can only repeat, remind, inspire, instruct, persuade, plead; the activity, the disciple must himself initiate. He must jump over the stile himself. No one can hoist him over it!

Mothers must assume this responsibility and not throw it on ayahs or governesses. Of course, ayahs and governesses are industrious and sincere. I have nothing to say against them. But, the child that is brought up by the ayah loses the essential fertilizer for growth, Love. The child is denied the most health giving vitamin, Love. The home where the fragrance of this love has to be inhaled has now lost its sacred atmosphere.

Without understanding what real meditation is, your attempts at meditation will result only in sound sleep. First of all try to understand the nature of the mind. Then only will you be able to control it. Once an old woman came to me and complained that her mind was giving her endless trouble by its restless wanderings. Then I asked her, "Where is that mind which is troubling you? Show it to me and I shall destroy it." She replied, "**Swami**, I don't know where it is." I told her, "If you do not know where the mind is, how do you say it is troubling you? Is it the mind that is troubling you or are you troubling yourself?" So without understanding anything about the mind, to blame it, is meaningless and to sit in meditation is sheer idleness. You must, therefore, have a thorough understanding of the nature of the mind as well as the senses. Everything in the world has some useful secrets to reveal. God does not create anything without a purpose. All things are purposeful, meaningful, blissful and valuable. But we are not making any effort to understand their mysteries.

Practice detachment from now on; practice it little by little, for a day will come sooner or later when you will have to give up all that you hold dear. Do not go on adding to the things which bind you to them. Bind yourself to the great liberator, God.

Time is changeless; it is the same in past, present, and future.
Come with empty hands and carry away My Love.
We are born in this world because we have forgotten God.

A true devotee will be steadfast in faith and pray to the Lord, not for **padartham** (things, material objects for the fulfillment of worldly desires), but for **pataartham**, the happiness that is super-worldly. When you manifest **Prema**, you are only expressing God, the Indweller of your Heart.

The Ten-Fold Path to Divinity

1. Love and serve the Motherland; do not hate or hurt the motherland of others.
2. Honor every religion; each is a path-way to the one God.
3. Love all men without distinction; know that mankind is a single community.
4. Keep your home and its environment clean; it will ensure health and happiness for you and for society.
5. Do not throw coins when beggars stretch their hands for alms; help them to become self-reliant. Provide food and shelter, love and care, for the sick and the aged.
6. Do not tempt others by offering bribes or demean yourself by accepting bribes.
7. Do not develop jealousy, hatred or envy on any account.
8. Do not depend on others to serve your personal needs; become your own servants before proceeding to serve others.
9. Observe the laws of the State and be an exemplary citizen.
10. Adore God. Abhor sin.

Lingham materialized by Sai Baba out of His mouth for this woman

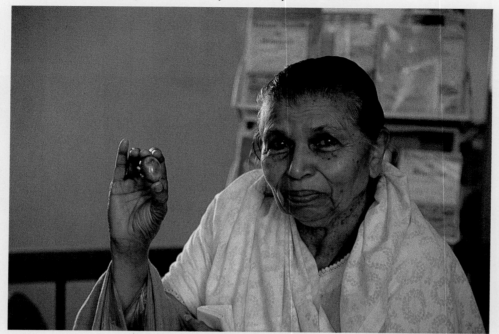

I am determined to correct you only after informing you of my credentials. That is why I am now and then announcing my Nature by means of miracles, that is, acts which are beyond human capacity and human understanding. Not that I am anxious to show off my powers. The object is to draw you closer to me, cement your hearts to me.

It is not possible for you to understand the divine purpose and gauge its potential or to know the fact that Divinity is among you, it becomes necessary for me to express this attitude of mine. Otherwise the atmosphere of hatred, greed, envy, cruelty, violence and irreverence will overwhelm the good, the humble, and the pious. The lingam is a symbol of the beginning-less and the endless, of the infinite ... it is the most fitting symbol of the Omnipresent, Omniscient, and Omnipotent Lord. Everything starts from it and everything is subsumed in it.

A million people sit cross-legged in meditation. Not one gains liberation from bondage. What is the point of it all?
If even the guru gains liberation, there might be some value. But even that does not happen. And if some slight
mistake is made, there is great harm. The net effect of it all is that it spoils both guru and disciple.
The apparent benefit is only temporary; it is not permanent.

Those who aspire to have mastery over the senses must have full faith in Me.

The devotee should look upon pain and pleasure alike as designed for his good.

A devotee should be ready to gladly accept anything as God's gift.

A moment of concentrated prayer from the heart is enough to melt and move God.

My **sankalpa** or Will confers bliss only after assessing the depth of yearning in the devotee. I, too, measure and weigh the sincerity and steadiness of the sadhana you have imposed upon yourself and I frame My sankalpa accordingly.

Tell them all to fulfill their assigned duties and responsibilities. The daily schedule of **puja, dhyana, bhajan, sankirtan** and study should be followed punctually and with faithful devotion.

Man is perpetually engaged in the search for peace. The seeker of peace must search for it not in religion (*matham*) but in the mind (*nmanam*). The search for peace in the external is the cause of all the unrest in the world. *Peace has to be established first within one's self. Then it has to be extended to the family. From the family, it has to spread to the village, the province, and the nation.* What is happening today is the reverse of this process. Conflict and disorder are spreading from the individual to the family and right up to the nation.

You sit in meditation for ten minutes after the evening **Bhajan** session; so far so good. But, let me ask, when you rise after the ten minutes and move about, do you see everyone in a clearer light as endowed with Divinity? If not, Meditation is a waste of time. Do you love more, do you talk less, do you serve others more earnestly? These are the signs of success in Meditation. Your progress must be authenticated by your character and behavior. Meditation must transmute your attitude towards beings and things, else it is a hoax. *Even a boulder will, through the action of sun and rain, heat and cold, disintegrate into mud and become food for a tree. Even the hardest heart can be softened so that the Divine can sprout therein.*

The body is the temple of God. The life of the person is the priest. The five senses are the vessels used in the religious ceremony. Atma is God, the idol of God. One cannot say that the body is the temple of God unless it is. Every act, thought and word should be worship in the temple. The five senses should be constantly cleansed and polished, so that the worship is reverently offered to God. One goes to the office and says to himself that every act of the day should be worship to God, and it will be so.

You sit in meditation for ten minutes after the evening **Bhajan** session; so far so good. But, let me ask, when you rise after the ten minutes and move about, do you see everyone in a clearer light as endowed with Divinity? If not, Meditation is a waste of time. Do you love more, do you talk less, do you serve others more earnestly? These are the signs of success in Meditation. Your progress must be authenticated by your character and behavior. Meditation must transmute your attitude towards beings and things, else it is a hoax. *Even a boulder will, through the action of sun and rain, heat and cold, disintegrate into mud and become food for a tree. Even the hardest heart can be softened so that the Divine can sprout therein.*

The body is the temple of God. The life of the person is the priest. The five senses are the vessels used in the religious ceremony. Atma is God, the idol of God. One cannot say that the body is the temple of God unless it is. Every act, thought and word should be worship in the temple. The five senses should be constantly cleansed and polished, so that the worship is reverently offered to God. One goes to the office and says to himself that every act of the day should be worship to God, and it will be so.

For a person, so small as to be invisible, so temporary in the expanse of the universe,
to live with his ego is shameful. Any person with ego is a disgrace.

Man is life with desire; life without desire is God.
Mind is desire; when mind disappears, desire disappears.

The Universe is a globe.
Earth and all beings are smaller globes within that.
The whole universe is held in Baba's hand.

Take the world as it is, never expect it to conform to your needs or standards. Maya envelopes the good with the blemish of the bad; it makes the evil glitter with the shine of the good. Discriminate to the best of your capacity, and develop the capacity to discriminate. Struggle to win, that is the best that you can do; few can say, "I have won." Your conscience knows the real source of joy; it will prod you towards the right path; your business is to take it as `guide' and not disobey it every time it contradicts your fancy.

Follow the master, the inside **Atma**, the super-conscious.

In walking, offer the action to the Lord to maintain a body fit for the Lord to live in; and that is the attitude for every single act of the day.

Step by step, you reach the end of the road. One act followed by another leads to a good habit. By listening, you get prodded into action. Resolve to act, to mix only in good company, to read only elevating books, to form the habit of **Namasmarana**-and then, **Ajnana** will vanish automatically. The **Anandam** that will well up within you by the contemplation of **Anandaswarupa** will drive out all grief, all worry.

A guru is a light to show one the road, but the destination is God. One is grateful to the guru, but it is God that one worships. Nowadays, one worships the guru, which is quite wrong.

The best way to determine whether or not a guru is genuine is if his words are full of wisdom and if in his life, he practices and is the same as his words. If the guru speaks only words of wisdom, and this is an age where people speak wisdom without being wise, the words of wisdom will produce no results whatsoever and are useless.

The best guru today is God.

God is in you, but like the woman who fears her necklace has been stolen or lost, recognizes that she has it round her neck when she passes a mirror, man too will recognize that God is in him, when some Guru reminds him of it.

The guru is that through which your minds gets attached to God. If you consider Supreme Consciousness as the guru and practice spiritual disciplines with unwavering love, the Lord himself will appear before you and give you instruction, just as a guru. Or, He may so bless you as a result of your intense devotion that you may meet a guru who is capable of initiating you into the highest truth.

The Lord has come in human form and moves about among men, so that He can be listened to, contacted, loved, revered and obeyed. He has to speak the language of men and behave like human beings, as a member of the species. Otherwise, He will be either negated and neglected or feared and avoided.

My teaching is love, my message is love, my activity is love, my way of living is love.

Love gives and forgives; ego gets and forgets.

Life is a challenge; fight to the end.
Life is a song; sing it.
Life is divine; realize it.
Life is character.
There is one path, complete life.

Once gone a day is gone forever.

Life sweeps along like a wild typhoon; the allotted years do melt like snow before the sun; but man wastes the precious chance, and strays into folly and frivolity. The yearning of the human soul, "From untruth lead me into Truth; from darkness lead me into Light; from death lead me into immortality," this is unrealized.

Glossaries

AJNANA, AJNANAM: Literally non-knowledge. Ignorance of the undying atma within man.

ANANDA, ANANDAM: Divine bliss; unending source of joy.

ANANDASWARUPA: Born to a rich heritage. Baba's nature is Ananda; Ananda is His sign.

ARJUNA: White, pure, unblemished unsullied. Arjuna was a hero of the Mahabharata (a famous Hindu epic) and the friend of Krishna.

ASHRAM, ASRAM: Hermitage of a spiritual personage. The retreat of a guru and his disciples to a place where man has no srama (struggle, bother, or effort).

ATMA, AATHMA: The unseen basis, the real Self, one's divinity. It is the spark of God within, one's own innermost reality.

AVATAR, AVATHAR: An incarnation of God in some form or other. The incarnation of the formless with form, for the uplift of human beings.

AVEDANA: Yearning for the Lord; anguished yearning.

AYAHS: Governess.

BALVIKAS: Spiritual education program for children; meaning awakening of the child.

BHAGAVAN: The Lord, God. It means He who possesses the six divine qualities in full: Omnipotence (omniscience and omnipresence); Dharma (equality, righteousness, justice); Splendor (glory, fame); Sri (prosperity, majesty, grace); Jnana (wisdom, enlightenment); Vairagya (detachment, tranquillity, equanimity).

BHAGAVATHCHINTHANA: Contemplation on the Lord.

BHAJAN, BHAJANA: Seeking our identity with the Lord through spiritual songs; a song in praise of God.

BHAKTA, BHAKTHA: One who is full of divine love and devotion to God. Steadfastness, faith and constancy are the characteristics of the bhakta.

BHAKTHI, BHAKTI: Devotion, dedication and absolute surrender to God. The state of mind in which one has no separate existence from God. Faith, fearlessness, and absence of egoism.

BODHA: Teaching.

BRAHMA: The Creator in Hindu Trinity. The personified Absolute.

BRAHMAN: The basic truth of the universe. Whatever is unchanging, eternally true. Brahman is indestructible; beyond time and space.

BRAHMANANDA: The bliss of Brahman itself.

CHIT: Full knowledge, awareness.

CHITTACHORA, CHITHTHACOR: Heart thief, Krishna, the stealer of hearts.

DAKSHINAMURTHI: Deity presiding over the human endeavor to acquire wisdom.

DAMODARA: The one with a rope around his waist. Refers to Sri Krishna when he was a young boy.

DHYANA: Meditation, contemplation, concentration. The practice of discipline; involves the development of truth, justice, peace and love.

DHAYANAYOGA: Inner discipline based on Sadhana (dedication to God) and Bhakthi(devotion).

GUNA, GUNAS: Human characteristics, qualities, attributes, types of behavior. There are three: Satva (good, noble, auspicious); Rajas (mere activity of dynamism); Thamas (darkness, ignorance, and inertia).

GURU: Teacher. Guide to spiritual liberation; one who removes ignorance. The word "GU" means darkness and ignorance, the word "RU" stands for the removal thereof.

JAPA: Recitation, continual repetition of the name of the Lord with surrender of ego and with devotion.

JAYA DEVA: Great poet devotee of Sri Krishna from eastern part of India.

JNANA THATWA: The light of wisdom.

KASI: Ancient city of Banaras

KARMA: Action, fate, destiny. The law that governs all action and its inevitable consequences on the doer. The law of cause and effect, of moral compensation for acts done in the past.

KATHOPANISHAD: One of ten invaluable text books on spiritual discipline and on the glorious fruit of spiritual adventure.

KRISHNA: He who draws you by means of the joy He imparts. Avatar of Lord Vishnu.

KRODA, KRODHA: Anger, resentment, hate. Yearning to harm others and bring them down in ruin.

LORD GOVINDA: Another name for Lord Krishna. One who looks after, tends, guards the cows. The inner meaning is one who has control over the animal nature in man.

MADHAVA: God, Lord of the universe. The Lord of Lakshmi, another name for Krishna.

MANTHRA: Chants, sacred words or formula. A form of spiritual initiation of an aspirant by his guru or guide.

MATHAM: Opinion, conclusion, point of view, religion.

MAYA: A mixture of fact and fiction. The primal illusion, the basic ignorance.

NAMASMARANA: Remembrance, recital. Constant repetition and reflection on the name of the Lord and the glory it seeks to express.

NARA: Creation, Man, Human.

NARAYANA: The primal person, the creator, the Lord Himself. He who resides in all beings, Vishnu.

NIRVANA: Liberation.

NISHKAMAKARMA, NISHKAAMA-KARMA: Activity engaged in as dedication and worship. Action without concern for any

benefit that may ensue.
NITHYAM: Permanent. That which is unaffected by the limitations of space, time and objectivisation. Indestructible.

PADARTHAM, PADARTHA, PADAARTHA: Objects for fulfillment of worldly desires.
PARAMATMA, PARAMATHMA, PARAMATMAN: The Universal Soul, God. The absolute from which everything has emanated, in which all exists.
PRAKRITI, PRAKRITHI: Nature, the world. Primordial nature which, in association with Purusha (eternal conscious principle) creates the universe.
PRANAYAMA: The inhaling and exhaling of the breath.
PRAPATHI: Dedication. The state of absolute self-surrender to the Highest.
PRASANTHI NILAYAM: The abode of undisturbed inner peace. The name of Sai Baba's ashram.
PRATYAHARA: Process where the mind is turned inward and away from external objects.
PREMA: Pure love which is unchanging, sincere, universal. Love for all beings prompting sacrifice of joys and comforts of oneself for the sake of insuring the joy and comfort of others.
PUJA: Ritual worship of the Lord. An offering at the Lotus Feet.
PUTTAPARTHI: The quiet and remote village in southern India where Sai Baba was born and where He now has His ashram.

RADHA: The beloved of KRISHNA. She symbolizes the total surrender of the soul to the Supreme Self.
RAMAKRISHNA PARAMAHANSA: Revered and Christ-like Indian master.

SADHAKA: One who is practicing the discipline of conquering his egoism and greed.
SADHANA: Spiritual discipline or practice through activities such as meditation and recitation of holy names. Exercise in sacrifice and surrender; involves dedication of all acts to God.
SAMSARA, SAMSAARA: The flowing pattern of life.
SAMSKARA: The tendencies inherent from previous births; life cycle rituals.
SANATHANA DHARMA: The ancient wisdom, the eternal path of righteousness.
SANDEHA: Doubt
SANKALPA BALA: Willpower motivated by God.
SANKALPA: Divine will; God's wish, grace. Something sought for, intention, desire, resolve.
SANKIRTAN: Reciting or singing with joy.
SANTHI: Undisturbed peace of mind. Can also be defined as the true prema towards the Lord, towards truth itself or towards true dharma (righteousness).
SARVABHUTHAANTHARAATMA: The inner reality of all beings. God. The soul immanent in every being.
SARVESWARA, SARVESVARA: The Lord of all, The source from which all power originates. The Supreme Sovereign.
SAT: Immortal existence, that which persists in the past, present and future, unaffected by time. The real, the essential.
SAT-CHIT-ANANDA: The cosmic being, awareness, bliss.
SATHSANGA: Company of the good, of the godly, and of the wise.
SATHYA, SATHYAM: Truth- that which is the same in the past, present, future.
SATHYA SAI: He who reclines on truth.
SATHYA SAI EHV: Education in human values. It is based on the values of truth, right action, peace, love and nonviolence. It stresses the importance of service to society, tolerance for people of different races, cultures, nationalities and religions.
SEVA: Service as worship of the divine around you; adoration of the Lord.
SHANTI, SHANTHI: Peace. Every being is in essence the embodiment of shanti. Our inner core is the realm of peace. Also, the absence of agitation or unrest.
SUTRA: String or verse.
SWAMI: Lord, spiritual preceptor.

UPADESH: Spiritual guidance.
UPANISHAD: Study and practice of the innate truth. A part of the Vedas; very important in the development of Hindu thought.

VAAK: Sound, voice; the words you speak.
VAIRAGYAM, VAIRAGYA: Detachment. Shedding your desires as you go up in the journey of life.
VEDANTA: Goal or finale of the Vedas, liberation.
VICHARA: Inquiry, discrimination, continuous self examination.
VITHACHORAS: Stealer of wealth.
VIVEKA: The capacity to reason and see things in proper proportion. Discrimination between the real and unreal, between the permanent and the not, between the beneficial and the not, between truth and falsehood.
VIVEKANANDA: A disciple of Ramakrishna Paramahamsa.

Bibliography

1. Baba, Bhagavan Sri Sathya Sai. <u>Geetha Vahini: The Divine Gospel</u>. Sri Sathya Sai Books and Publications Trust. Prasanthi Nilayam, India.

2. Baba, Bhagavan Sri Sathya Sai. <u>Sadhans: the Inward Path</u>. Sri Sathya Sai Books and Publications Trust. Prasanthi Nilayam, India.

3. Baba, Bhagavan Sri Sathya Sai. <u>Dhyana Vahini: Practice of Meditation</u>. Sri Sathya Sai Books and Publications Trust. Prasanthi Nilayam, India.

4. <u>Teachings of Sri Satya Sia Baba</u>. Sathya Sai Book Center of America. 1974.

5. Murphet, Howard. <u>Sia Baba Avatar: A New Journey Into Power and Glory</u>. Macmillan India Limited. Madras. 1993.

6. <u>Summer Showers in Brindavan, 1990</u>. Sri Sathya Sai Books and Publications Trust. Prasanthi Nilayam, India.

7. Kasturi, N. <u>Sathya Sai Baba: Part IV</u>. Sri Sathya Sai Books and Publicaations Trust. Prasanthi Nilayam, India. American Printing 1988.

8. Baba, Bhagavan Sri Sathya Sai. <u>Sathya Sai Speaks: Sathya-Dharma-Shaanthi-Prema Vol. IV</u>. Sri Sathya Sai Books and Publications Trust. Andhra Pradesh, India.

9. Hislop, Dr. John S. <u>My Baba and I</u>. Birth Day Publishing Company. San Diego, CA. 1985.

10. Hislop, Dr. John S. <u>Conversations With Sathya Sai Baba</u>. Birth Day Publishing Company. San Diego, CA. 1978.

11. <u>Sanathana Sarathi</u>. Sai Sathya Sai Books and Publications Trust. Prasanthi Nilayam. Vol. 38 No. 2. Feb.1995.

12. Murphet, Howard. <u>Where the Road Ends: From Self Through Sai to Self.</u> Leela Press Inc. Faber, VA. 1994.

13. Edited by Dr. Bhagavantam. <u>Summer Showers in Brindavan 1978</u>. Sri Sathya Sai Education & Publication Foundation. India. 1978.

14. Compiled by Brahmanand Mavinkurve. <u>Namasmarana: A Universal Sadhana</u>. Sai Sathya Sai Books & Publications Trust. Andhra Pradesh, India.

15. Pamphlet. <u>Sathya Sai Baba</u>. Sathya Sai Book Center of America. Tustin, CA.

16. Sandweiss, Samuel H., M.D. <u>Spirit and the Mind</u>. Birth Day Publishing Company. San Diego, CA. 1985.

17. Eruch B. Fanibunda. <u>Vision of the Divine.</u> Sri Sathya Sai Books & Publications Trust, Bombay, India.1987.

18. Shah, I. <u>We Devotees.</u> Sathya Sia Book center of America. Tustin, CA.

19. <u>Sanatana Sarathi</u> Vol. 37 Sri Sathya Sia Books and Publications Trust. Prasanthi Nilayam. Nov. 1994 No. 11.

20. <u>Sanathan Sarathi</u> Vol. 37. Sri Sathya Sia books and Publications Trust. Prasanthi Nilayam. Dec. 1994 No. 12.

Books of publications are available at
Sathya Sai Book Center of America
305 West First Street
Tustin California 92680
Tel: 714 669 0522
Fax: 714 669 9138